ON MY WAY TO LIBERATION

The BreakBeat Poets Series

ABOUT THE BREAKBEAT POETS SERIES

The BreakBeat Poets series, curated by Kevin Coval and Nate Marshall, is committed to work that brings the aesthetic of hip-hop practice to the page. These books are a cipher for the fresh, with an eye always to the next. We strive to center and showcase some of the most exciting voices in literature, art, and culture.

BREAKBEAT POETS SERIES TITLES INCLUDE:

The BreakBeat Poets: New American Poetry in the Age of Hip-Hop, edited by Kevin Coval, Quraysh Ali Lansana, and Nate Marshall

This is Modern Art: A Play, Idris Goodwin and Kevin Coval

The BreakBeat Poets Vol 2: Black Girl Magic, edited by Mahogany Browne, Jamila Woods, and Idrissa Simmonds

Human Highlight, Idris Goodwin and Kevin Coval

On My Way to Liberation, H. Melt

Black Queer Hoe, Britteney Black Rose Kapri

Citizen Illegal, José Olivarez

Graphite, Patricia Frazier

The BreakBeat Poets Vol 3: Halal if You Hear Me, edited by Fatimah Asghar and Safia Elhillo

There are Trans People Here, H. Melt

Commando, E'mon Lauren

ON MY WAY TO LIBERATION

H. Melt

Haymarket Books
Chicago, IL

Published in 2018 by
Haymarket Books
P.O. Box 180165
Chicago, IL 60618
www.haymarketbooks.org

ISBN: 978-1-60846-592-7

Trade distribution:
In the US, Consortium Book Sales and Distribution, www.cbsd.com
In Canada, Publishers Group Canada, www.pgcbooks.ca
In the UK, Turnaround Publisher Services, www.turnaround-uk.com
All other countries, Ingram Publisher Services International,
IPS_Intlsales@ingramcontent.com

This book was published with the generous support of Lannan Foundation and Wallace
Action Fund.

Cover design by River Kerstetter.

Printed in the United States by union labor.

10 9 8 7 6 5 4 3 2 1

To River

You are on your way.

CONTENTS

INTRODUCTION: ON SEARCHING FOR TRANS LIBERATION

When my grandfather Pa Howie learned that I am a writer, he told me to tell his story. This was a surprising request, considering that he often tells his own story, providing a firsthand account of surviving the Holocaust to schools, museums, and community centers. Growing up, I was always proud of his willingness to share his story so that future generations will never forget. In this way, he taught me the power of using personal narratives as a political tool.

This chapbook connects our stories and lives. We share a history of fighting for liberation. The title poem reveals that my grandfather crossed gender lines as an act of survival. Being trans is integral to my survival. For both of us, telling our stories is an act of liberation. I hope that our recounting of painful memories leads to a less violent future.

In these poems, I reflect on the ways cis people have failed me. I write about the erasure of trans identity in public and private spaces—in the sex shop, my workplace, and my home. I transition from talking about cis people and how they've harmed me, to directly addressing trans people and envisioning trans liberation.

I am in the strange position of being an openly trans writer while simultaneously not being recognized as a trans person on a daily basis. I struggle with this dissonance regularly. Misrecognition does not only occur in straight spaces. It happens within gay and lesbian spaces too. I yearn for trans spaces within the cis world and try to imagine living outside of it. How do you envision trans liberation while living in a cis world?

I surround myself with trans people. I read trans books and watch trans movies. I dance and march with trans friends. I hang a trans flag in my window. I paint my nails pink and blue. I eat a cupcake at the trans bakery. I see a trans affirming therapist. I write about it. Because my writing is where I feel most free.

-H. Melt

TRANS LIT IS BULLSHIT

After Jamila Woods

Trans Lit is bullshit unless it is written
by trans people, unless it is written
for trans people. I want Trans Lit
that breaks linear narrative.
I want Trans Lit to bash back
against the police. I want Trans Lit
to take up an entire bookshelf
in the library. I want Trans Lit
in every classroom, in every backpack,
in every pair of hands on a long commute.
I want Trans Lit not to be a federal crime.[1]
I want Trans Lit in prisons, to set my
brothers, sisters, and siblings free.

---

1   In 2015, Chelsea Manning was facing solitary confinement, partially due to a "prohib-
    ited property" charge related to books and magazines that were found in her cell and
    confiscated, including Casey Plett's book *A Safe Girl to Love*.

TO BE A BODY

to be a body
not come out
of your body

to be a body
not be in
your body

to be a body
to be a no
body

to be a body
no body
sees

to be a body
no body
believes.

A PAIR OF SHOES

i'm sitting on a bench
waiting for the train

a man sits next to me
and compliments my
purple shoes

where did you get those?
i take my headphones off

his tone and
his body
shift

he tells me
i'm gay too
i like girls too

as he invites himself
to stroke my arms
and thighs

i tell him
i'm not gay
i'm trans

the distinction
doesn't matter
to him

i'm just a body
i'm just a pair
of shoes

dangling
in front
of him.

HAPPY HOLIDAYS

Hi, you've reached H. Melt.
I can't come to the phone right now.
If you leave a message, I'll get back to you
as soon as possible. Thanks.

>Hi Hannah,
>it's Nana calling.
>
>I wanted to thank you for that lovely note
>with good wishes for Hannukah and the New Year.
>I really appreciate it. I was delighted to hear from you.
>
>Mother tells me your opening went really well.
>I wanted to wish you luck with that.
>I hope you sell a lot of books
>and make a lot of money.
>
>If you get a chance, call me.
>If not, I know you're a
>Busy. Young. Woman.
>
>I'm thinking of you and wish you the best.
>Thank you again for that lovely note
>and have a happy holiday.

THANKSGIVING MEAL

i arrive at my parents house
for my first thanksgiving
with my girlfriend

in the oven is the turkey
on the stove are green beans
in the fish shaped pan jello molds

i am first to fill my plate
and sit at the long table
where we pretend
to be one

my sisters husband
squeezes next to me
our elbows and knees
kissing

he calls me
by the wrong
name

as if eight months ago
h. melt didn't appear
on my place card
at his wedding

as if i am not
part of the family
that loves him now.

ODE TO THE ARQUETTE FAMILY

The Arquettes
are a classic
hollywood
family

when Alexis passed
they publicly
mourned

talked to media outlets
without misgendering
or deadnaming her

in a dream after
Alexis passed
Patricia said

I come from the future
I'm your sister
I love you so much

my own sister lives
in the past, never says
I love you even a little

I dream of a sister who
isn't afraid of embrace
who loves me before
I'm gone.

ODE TO THE GAY SEX SHOP

Man's Country is closing
The Bijou already shut
where will gay men go
for anonymous sex
in Chicago

i go to Full Kit Gear
my trans flag and pronoun
buttons proudly displayed

when they grab the nipple clamps
from behind the counter it's *she*
when i leave it's *thanks guys*
even though i'm alone

i could've gone
to the feminist sex shop
where the owner has pink hair
and a trans kid but their products
aren't as cute

i feel home
at both places
home meaning
misrecognition.

MEETING EILEEN MYLES

"Thanks for the fine intro & your supreme queer lesbian taste & existence"
–Eileen Myles

on halloween
i dressed up as john waters
to introduce eileen myles
at women & children first

a huge crowd gathered
as they read *an american poem*
and a few about dogs

afterwards
i passed out candy
to people in the
signing line

when i handed them
my copy of *chelsea girls*
they inscribed it
to a lesbian

to someone
who does
not exist

except in their
imagination.

FAGGOT WITH FLOWERS

In the summertime
I walk to the farmers market
on my lunch break from work

most of the vendors are queer
selling tomatoes and peaches
empanadas, cider and curds

I spy brain flowers, which my mom
occasionally bought, though
she favored gladiolas

I debate whether or not
to buy flowers, they're
not food, a bit of a luxury

as I walk back to work
proudly holding
my cockscombs

a grey pickup truck blows
a stop sign, presses
the gas in my path

he cracks the window
to yell faggot at me
missing my body

I go home and place
my flowers in water
on the kitchen table

trying to forget
what will die
in a few days
time.

TO ALL THOSE LISTENING

"From the way the general description of the apartment has been provided me,
some items may not be 'suitable for viewing' by the public at-large, especially any
minor children which would possibly accompany their parents."
—A. Steve Warnelis, Property Manager, XL Properties

When I found the letter
hung with blue tape
on my front door
I ran outside

my girlfriend
waiting in the car
to take me away
from my home

I couldn't sleep
in my own bed, eat in my
own kitchen, ride the train
without thoughts of jumping

my apartment walls
said *no hetero*, said
buttfuck the binary
said *I am alive*

my family said *medicate*
said *history of depression*
said *this isn't discrimination*

my lawyer says *illegal*
my therapist says *trauma*
I say *help* and I say *thanks*
to all those listening
answering my calls.

THERE ARE TRANS PEOPLE HERE

After Jamaal May

There are trans people here,
so many trans people here
is what I am trying to say.

When they say we are all
trapped in the wrong body
impostor, impossible. No.

We are on the bus
next to you. In the
cubicle next to you.
In the check out line
next to you.

Some of us are sex workers,
teachers, artists, nurses,
homeless, unemployed
and hungry too.

We are as real
and complicated
as anyone else.

But they won't stop murdering.
Stop legislating. Stop imprisoning.
Stop claiming we are ruining our
countries, families, friendships
and futures too.

When every day
we awaken to
build them
anew.

MEETING CHELSEA MANNING

After the Lambda Literary Awards

"Why do we still need to be 'explained' by a cisgender person with fancy titles,
awards, and credentials?" –Chelsea Manning

I'm bored at an after party
in manhattan, the dj is bad
no one is dancing & only
the vodka is free

I notice poets sitting
in the corner: Sam &
Franny & Cam & William
tells me Chelsea is here
I don't believe him
but it's true

there's a circle around her
the host Mx. Justin Vivian Bond
the lawyer Chase Strangio
the journalist from vogue
the documentary filmmaker

I introduce myself
as a writer & ask
what she read
in solitary

I don't know this is
her first night out
since release

I already know, we've both
read *Nevada*, I already know
we've both considered suicide
like most trans people, I know.

IF YOU ARE OVER CIS PEOPLE

After Morgan Parker

Don't kill yourself.
Make trans friends.
Schedule an appointment at
Chicago Women's Health Center.

Don't watch or listen to fox news.
Search for Janet Mock's writing
on the internet or the shelves
at Unabridged or Bluestockings.

Don't stay at a transphobic job
or apologize when you are
misgendered or misnamed
by family or friends.

Don't go home
for the holidays.
Cook your own feast.
Set your own table.

Use the bathroom
when you need it.
Don't hold it in.

TRANS PEOPLE DON'T WANT TO BE YOUR FRIEND

25% of americans
don't want to be friends
with a trans person

100% of trans people
don't want to be
your friend

we're not here
for your comfort
your panels or
tokenization

we are here
for cracking cis jokes
finding each other jobs
teaching your children
how to embrace
their full selves

less than 20% of cis people
are open to dating
our sexy selves

I don't want to date
99.9% of cis people
I don't need any
new friends

all I want is a love
that doesn't end
in a headline.

CITY OF TRANS LIBERATION

After Martín Espada

Where statues of Lou
and Sylvia dance
in the streets

Where no kids are
kicked out or run
away from home

Where no body
asks for ID or
our *real* names

Where every body
has a body they
believe in

Where we walk outside
in the daytime without
being harassed

Where we are taught
to love instead of kill
ourselves

Where Trans Day of Remembrance
celebrates those who died
of natural causes

Where there are
no borders between
who we were and who we are

Becoming.

ON MY WAY TO LIBERATION

For Pa Howie

I'm on the train
wearing a pink shirt
and floral tie

on the way to celebrate
my grandfather's liberation
from dachau

when the nazis
came for his family
in kovno, lithuania

my grandfather
dressed like a girl
to stay close to his
mother and sisters

when he immigrated
to the united states
he changed his name
from *michelson* to *melton*

I've changed my name
and my clothes too
on my way to
liberation.

ACKNOWLEDGEMENTS

On My Way to Liberation is a preview of the forthcoming book *There Are Trans People Here*. This chapbook was edited by Kevin Coval. Thank you to the journals that previously published the poems noted below:

The Feminist Wire: "Thanksgiving Meal"

Heart Journal: "Ode to the Gay Sex Shop" & "On My Way to Liberation"

Lambda Literary: "City of Trans Liberation"

The Offing: "To Be a Body"

Vinyl: "A Pair of Shoes"

The following poems inspired several of the pieces in this collection: "Blk Girl Art" by Jamila Woods, "There Are Birds Here" by Jamaal May, "If You Are Over Staying Woke" by Morgan Parker, and "The Republic of Poetry" by Martín Espada.

Thank you to everyone in my life who's helped me on my way to liberation. A few of those people include: Nate Marshall, Jamila Woods, Fatimah Asghar, José Olivarez, Britteney Kapri, Plus Sign, Danez Smith, Morgan Parker, Angel Nafis, Shira Erlichman, Oli Rodriguez, Reese Kelly, Beyza Ozer, River Kerstetter, Sylvie Lydon, Bea Cordelia, Logan Pierce, Janie Stamm, Nancy Segal, David Melton, Fred Sasaki, Ydalmi Noriega, the staff at Women & Children First, and the staff at Haymarket Books, especially Jim Plank and Julie Fain.

ABOUT THE AUTHOR

H. Melt is a poet, artist, and educator whose work proudly celebrates Chicago's queer and trans communities. Their writing has appeared many places including the *Chicago Reader, The Offing,* and *Them,* the first trans literary journal in the United States. They are the author of *The Plural, The Blurring* and editor of *Subject to Change: Trans Poetry & Conversation.* Lambda Literary awarded them the Judith A. Markowitz Award for Emerging LGBTQ Writers. They've also been named to *Newcity's* Lit 50 list, as well as *Windy City Times'* 30 under 30. H. Melt co-leads Queeriosity at Young Chicago Authors and works at Women & Children First, Chicago's feminist bookstore.

CPSIA information can be obtained
at www.ICGtesting.com
Printed in the USA
JSHW011443290822
29736JS00001B/1